Poets' Corner 2019

The Bayside Writers' Group

Copyright © 2019
The Bayside Writers' Group
All Rights Reserved
ISBN: 978-0-6485152-3-4

This publication may not be reproduced, stored in a retrieval system, or transmitted in whole or in part, in any form or by any means, electronic, mechanical, photocopying, recording, or otherwise without the consent of the author(s). Inquiries should be addressed to the publisher.

Published in Australia
Printed by Ingram Spark

Poets' Corner 2019

Authors: Ann Simic, Judith Dowling, Foti, Suzanne Siebert, Andrew Lewis, Amanda Divers, Peter Levy, Elizabeth MacGregor

Design: Alex Nutman
a.e.nutman@gmail.com

Acknowledgements

I would like to thank all those who took the time to submit their works to us.
Please note that if anyone would like to make contact with any of the poets in this collection that the best way would be to either post a letter:

The Bayside Writers' Group
22 Stradbroke Avenue
Brighton East, Victoria, Australia 3187

Or email:

peter@peterlevy.com.au

CONTENTS

Birth - 1
Ann Simic

Secrets of the Vicar's wife - 3
Judith Dowling

Miss me - 5
Foti

Bruised Tranquility - 7
Suzanne Siebert

An aching smile - 9
Andrew Lewis

Anticipate - 10
Amanda Divers

The same mistakes - 11
Peter Levy

A to Z - 12
Elizabeth MacGregor

The Lake - 14
Ann Simic

Russian Sonya - 15
Judith Dowling

Perfection Vanishes - 16
Foti

Gemini- 17
Suzanne Siebert

Last night- 19
Andrew Lewis

Chances aren't for the weak- 20
Amanda Divers

I am the blame- 21
Peter Levy

I am pausing- 22
Elizabeth MacGregor

A Sestina for the fence- 23
Ann Simic

Depression in the south annex- 25
Judith Dowling

Request- 28
Foti

Moon- 29
Suzanne Siebert

Like a ripple in some stream- 32
Andrew Lewis

Clap back- 33
Amanda Divers

I hear silence all the time- 34
Peter Levy

I intermingle with the living - 35
Elizabeth MacGregor

Speak to me - 36
Ann Simic

The Biographer - 37
Judith Dowling

Taste is everything - 39
Foti

Testing the water - 41
Suzanne Siebert

If she only knew - 43
Andrew Lewis

I had a dream - 44
Amanda Divers

Still there - 45
Peter Levy

None but the brave - 46
Elizabeth MacGregor

In the pink on the Mexican/US border - 47
Ann Simic

Belles De Jour - 48
Judith Dowling

Erase my mind - 50
Foti

Shadows - 51
Suzanne Siebert

Who am I? - 52
Andrew Lewis

The devil cries - 53
Amanda Divers

Just now! Just you! - 54
Peter Levy

Perhaps - 55
Elizabeth MacGregor

Birth

For Sunny Bell Simic

Parting from the interior,
a new beginning on the outside
recalling the same rhythms,
the pulses that sang with you
for so long in your safe chamber.

And he who mapped your journey,
fellow travellers,
drifting into sleep
against his cheek, embedded in his
embrace after the night of labour
he shared with you two.

Detached, uncoupled from your
lifeline into the arms of love, sailing
on your own sea, sun and air
guiding your new chapter,
the moon cycling into your cycle.

Your family of forces across the air-
waves, throbbing in harmony,
lighting your intrepid history:
dawn ushered you into a rich,
intricate and puzzling tapestry.

They gaze into your eyes whose
colour will reveal itself, whose
focus will form to feel, to see the
impact of a smile, a word, a song
and seize them for her own.

In a new guise, spin your own yarn,
play your own tune, crawl, walk,
run into the unknown, unknowable
future, space-time overflowing,
cupped in the curve of love.

Ann Simic

Secrets of the Vicar's wife

My mother believed in dyeing
And in the resurrection
She dyed in the boiling copper in the laundry
To camouflage jumble sale clothes
Into a church bazaar of colours
Then she'd shorten or lengthen
Take in, take out and tuck over
Reverse, remodel, reshape, redrape
And swap the buttons
Nothing suspect
No-one ever knew.

"Well, hello and welcome Mrs Umdear
I do like the hat you're wearing.
What is it I spy you have here?
Ah nice apple pie! How very caring
Ah my dear, let me make it clear
That the Vicar will be delighted."

My mother wore a different hat to Matins
And another for Evensong
Each week, for years and years.
When she ran to catch the butcher
Who closed up on the dot of five
Or when she had gone to her painting classes
Or went to a very smart wedding
She put on a revamped hat, a dress or a jacket
From the parish church jumble sale
Nobody ever knew.

Garnered from the grandest, richest and fairest
Ladies of the church congregation.
From Mrs Um and Miss Er Er,
The bank manager's wife and the lawyer's wife too
And from the women who travelled the world
Hats would be folded, flowered and flounced
Ribboned, ruffled, and rolled
They sat on her head with a brand new twist
So as she fervently knelt on Sundays
She couldn't help but silently chuckle
Knowing her hat was greatly admired
And that nobody ever knew.

Judith Dowling

Miss me

Miss the things I used to be
Miss the way I used to feel
Miss friends who were so real

Then I didn't know what I wanted to be
I didn't know I was happy
still I wish that I could find
that part of me I knew was mine

I'm growing old
my emotions have gone cold
too much sorrow, too much pain
leaves me no reason to remain

All my colours have turned to grey
and old photographs seem to say
I'll be with you at your side
I'm the past you cannot hide

I miss me
miss the way I used to be
remembering when I was young
when loving life was so much fun.

All the dreams I thought I'd see
turn into reality
have all been washed away –
tell me why should I stay?

Times when I pause
and look around at what I see,
remembering days when I was young
that's when I start missing me.

there was once a sparkle in my eye
for the things I'd love to do

now I don't, or won't
instead wasting time through rhyme.

Foti

Bruised Tranquility

Today hits hard and I wear the bruises, blackness of burden and purple bruises of sorrow
Sorrow, I'm still dealing with it today, and it's already there for tomorrow
Did you see me leave or notice that I'm gone; leaving to find something else I can follow
Something like tomorrow, you might get close to me, what I need is tranquility
Before we move too far away from each other, in another messy conversation on the phone
That is too familiar, I'm just another messy complication, and my bruises show
1ooo miles of hurt and thought, strangely keep us bound yet completely removed from each other
There's no escape either; there's not enough time, because those chances are too narrow
Why is there always so much of never enough? My eyes have changed, looking still, so young, yet so very lost
Tomorrow, let me be, let me see, let me forget how it got this way, let me stay, how bad could it be
Even though you're distant, can't you keep me? Just In your heart, or just set me apart
You've taken the high ransom; so at least take me at random,
Can I be next, or is there a line, or do I need to wait til I lose even more time
I'm not even going to blink, not even stop for at least a last glance
To see a revelation coming, cos I already know its marching straight past

Bruise upon emotional bruise, I wear too many scars from feeling,
Only part of me lives here, things that were meant for me, did they leave, or just never arrive?
Is there a door I should I knock on, should I call again, or are they even here?
If I phone it only went to answer, no question about that, not even later
I need just a little, of little things, the ones that don't just ache or sting
Bruise upon emotional bruise, I wear too many scars from feeling
I'm only asking to find a way to be, without a bruised tranquility, cos that's all I need

Suzanne Siebert

An aching smile

An aching smile of knowing
Years of nothing new
Lover's touch of memory
Curses right on cue.
The look within the distance
Indifferent to the eye
Pointless evils in the gaze
I see my life drift by.
I feel my life drift by.
I know my life drifts by.

Andrew Lewis

Anticipate

Blue eyed beauty, with a heart of gold

right hand hook that stings with the
resemblance of a scorpion
topaz flickers through her eyes

kindred spirit of two that neglects to grow old

a kindness that would make the angels cry

my pride in her could be challenged to that of a lion

some have called her reckless,
others have called her naive

I'd prefer to say she is in love with the
anticipation of life
she lives it the way it's mean to be.

Amanda Divers

The same mistakes

I know I make the same mistakes
Comparing others to myself
The arrogance of my stance is unfounded
There is nothing to be judged by me.
I hide among the memories
No sun lights this way
Oh you cold wind of regret
Can't you see I am content?
A glaring stillness beckons,
I would always respond
But not for you, my love,
The shadows are just shadows.
You know my naked truth
Pain touches one and then all
Forever in your debt
As sleep attempts again.

Peter Levy

A to Z

An able Adam avoided anger
Bravely blessed by beauty beyond blemish
Collectively chosen creatures craved co-habitation
Desiring duties, defending defenceless demons
Eventually engineering Eden's eternal eviction
Fame for fury's fortune? Fortune for forgotten fame?
Given greatness, grace, gold, God?
Heaven's hotel, hereafter heralded
Ill-informed ideals, incinerate in isolation
Justice, joked juries, judged jealously
Kindly kings, kill, knowingly
Lingering lies languish, leaving latent love lost
Men's merriment marches midst mechanised machinery
Newer numbers numb, nutrients, now nearly none
Organizations order overhauls on obvious oversights
Peasantry priced purchased paraphernalia performs poorly
Quality quietly quietened quite quickly
Removing rightful reason, religiously, returning ruin
Soul sapping sorrow seduces some shallow soldiers
Taming temptation triumphs terribly this time
Unrelenting, under unjust utilizations, usually useless
Valuable victories, vanquished victors vanish vainly

Written words work warfare, while we wonder why
Xenaphobia, 'xplainations 'xcluded
Your young yelling youths yielding yesterday's yapping
Zealously zoned zombies, zapping zealots …. zero
Ah, almost admired, amid all ancient attitudes
But blinded, bungled, broken below bulging bellies.

Elizabeth MacGregor

The Lake

The breeze touches the water's surface,
whispers warm embraces, smoothly
beguiles the waiting water into a swoon.
The moon enfolds the frothing waves
in its cocoon, licks the whirling liquid;
the lake sighs and moans, murmurs
with fervour on the brink of opening
its arms to cling, to clasp, to clutch.
Mountainous mounds surround the water,
weakening its knees, trees shaft erect
upright to the sky and fly into a frenzy.
They growl and howl, birds shriek and screech.
Cumulous clouds hump and swell until
their breath subsides and hush descends.

Ann Simic

Russian Sonya

I suppose you are dead now Russian Sonya
You must be so dreadfully old
I read about you in the Daily News
Just a few lines – and then you were gone
Seems like you just didn't matter to us
After all you had lived your life
In your country afar, in terrible strife
I am left to make scratchy pictures.

If you survived Russian Sonya
How are you?
The newspaper didn't say.

You were old even then, poor Sonya
When they bludgeoned the life out of you
Darkly draped in your faith
In the Church of the Holy Annunciation
I supposed you clutched to your breast
A little gold cross, as you prayed.
Did you stay in this world for long enough
To know that they had shattered your head,
When your blood flowed onto the feet
Of a marble Virgin Mary?
Did she look sweetly down at you?
And Sonya, tell me this
Was that smile for you?

Judith Dowling

Perfection Vanishes

I paint the world black with my tongue
Speaking careless words
spray painting dark emotions over other's feelings,
Ruining their day,
Eroding their fondness of me all the more.
Self destructively I pace ever forwards.
Destructive thoughts, voices, memories,
Dismembering my soul,
Tearing apart my fragile pretence at holding it together.
Longing a world of false realities,
Oh to escape harsh self truths.
I anesthetise my mind with sermons inside earphones
And quell the storms within.
The morning is quiet after the mind's storms
And I look out at life's bleak remains.
Our life could have been so much more,
if not for me,
If not for circumstances,
If not for others using us for their own egos and agendas.
I lay on the remains of a couch
Allow my weary eyelids to rest
And search to feel again that I'm in a perfect world.
That I can grab part of that place
And drag it into my reality.
As I open my eyes,
Perfection vanishes.

Foti

Gemini

Gemini keeps an exciting mystic duality, wanting to run, to chase, to see and then catch life
Ideas are as wild and big as you believe them to be, you don't hesitate
To assess, or to just wait and see, you are a solo traveler, with two frames of mind
Curious, sometimes cautious, other times not as Gemini's nature will always tease you to try
You have so much to say, and you talk as fast as you think
You're prepared for anything random that calls 'this is where you'll feel free'
But the complexity is that you realize that you are tempted to fly
Just when refreshing cool waters are singing 'swim deep'
You love the impossible, but don't look when you leap
Gemini, your strength is your will and that is your streak
Your nature is to explore and be found at the same time
But you can't be in both places, and you don't like to be still
There are no warnings for Gemini, one minute you're blowing out candles
The next second you're holding your breath
You don't touch the bottom whilst cutting your cake
In case birthday wishes will sink as fast as they're made, and which ones you will keep
For you will change them again, that is your nature

You are a 'Gentle one' of elements and sensitive to all, you are whoever you are at 'one moment'
A chameleon of colours with every sense vibrant and awake
You set no expectations because everything could change
You have searched for something called reason and there is one you will find
The birthright of wonder and instinct, precious Gemini child

Suzanne Siebert

Last night

Last night was filled with broken sleep
A restless mind of endless schemes
Where all my best intentions live
And stay well hidden inside dreams.
What I'd do with Lotto's loot
To glean a look that can't be bought
When easing debts of family friends
With casualness that champions sport.
The hero's journey strong and true
Whatever demon shows its head
Admiring eyes on cool bravado
Saving all, while still in bed
Awake with tired mind and limbs
Still yearning for a minute more
And yet, the challenge of this day
Is blessed by all that went before.

Andrew Lewis

Chances Aren't For The Weak

Take chances people say

Frontal headaches plaguing me
 sleeping problems
I can't breathe
Help me
Stop.
It's 3 am
I wander the house again.
I am desperate to be loved
And just like that another lie is spun
It flashes in, in forms of names, catalogues and stories
I am wounded
The moment you walk away I'll shove you through that door.

I don't want to love you anymore.

Amanda Divers

I am the blame

Life is sold, and love is bought
I am the blame
And I weep into my constant thought
Of that, that is, and has no name.
What was of me has long since gone
I am the pain
What point, I ask, of even being born?
No choice, no choice, you say, again.
I feel no warmth in tired sleeps
I am the blame
Tormented souls tossed onto countless heaps
All at peace, all the same.
And where are you in all of this?
I am the blame, I am still here
You are my friend, some part of me
That needs your love right now and near.
Too easily I drift in rage
I am the pain
Always fearful of the day
Holding thoughts within my brain.
I am the blame.

Peter Levy

I am pausing

The things you say you know of me
Only reinforce how little and narrow it is
Decades of monologue without listening
Aeons of observance without seeing.
Each of us so full of our own importance
Avoiding intimacy as too threatening.
I am pausing now so as not to miss you
My journey is ever so richer for it.

Elizabeth MacGregor

A Sestina for the Fence

The palings are falling like rotten teeth.
Gape toothed, it flaps in the breeze
held up by wandering vines and leaf debris.
The fence and I chat with each other:
"Stand up straight," I smile, stretching myself
but the fence is quite happy to sway and bend.

The fencers want to knock it down and bend
their backs until it sparkles like false teeth,
but I'm not so sure myself:
the fence and I like to shoot the breeze
over wine. Could you do that with the other
all straight and formal minus old debris.

I wander over to remove debris
but the fence screams at me and bends
precariously. "Sorry," I say, vowing to wait for another
day, feeling guilt at its chattering teeth,
worried it could keel over in the slightest breeze,
knowing I'll have no one to blame but myself.

I've always like old things myself,
the friendliness of dishevelled debris,
to reminisce as words waft on the breeze
and lift me to a place where my mind bends
to a time I liked to cut my teeth
on one thing and another.

I'm quite happy to entertain the other
but never want to discard old friends myself.
Worn by time, we can still get our teeth
into debate and sweep away the mind's debris
so all our posts and palings bend
and extend ideas to fly upon the breeze.

With this plan in mind we'll breeze
through life, the old along with the other,
flexible to the very end, we'll bend
the rules as I have done myself
but my neighbour raves about debris:
I smile, acquiesce, don't bare my teeth.

I clean my teeth, across the fence the other,
watch the breeze sweep tendrils of debris
away. Bend for the end myself.

Ann Simic

Depression in The South Annex

"Depression. One forty five. South Annex. Bring paper and pen."
It's Jenny's birthday. How old do you think? Forty?
Nah, fifty if she's a day I reckon. She's got hairs on her chin
You going to depression?
Nah, too tired.
Cups and plates. All over the place. Mess, mess, mess. Scattered everywhere.
Frank you're jabbering
Sorry Mick sorry sorry. But look, cups an' plates all over over over. Sorry but I get upset.
Frank's a bit upset Kathy
Here Frank have a bicky. Give him a bicky Mick. Coffee creams
I reckon he'll be worse tomorrow. Always bad on Thursdays
I like your boobs Kathy
Well good for you Michael. Who's got the cake?
Come on Jenny, get your cake from the fridge
Can't be bothered with the silly cake. You get it Norm.
Frank says he hates chocolate cake
More for us hey Kathy

Don't just look at it. Frank. You're supposed to sing the birthday song
I hate the stupid birthday song Jenny
Frank hates everything does'n he just
You lot are doing my head in. just cut the cake.
I'm cutting the wretched cake Mike. Get off ya bum and hand it out

I bet it's just like mum used to didn't make
My mother was a rat
Oh sorry to hear that Frank. Here Luv have another bicky
There, now you've done it. You've got me thinking about my mum
Not to worry Jenny. Listen to me, you're a very nice person.
Far from it. You forgot to put the candle on the cake Frank
Thanks for that Kathy
Sorry sorry sorry Jenny.
I'll light the candle for you Luv and we'll sing the birthday song. Ok?
Hurry up or we'll be late for depression
Hey the ruddy candle's singing. Must have some psych problem
I'm sorry but I don't sing. Hate singing. Sorry.
Ya have to sing the song Frank
Doesn't matter Frank.
It's lovely, isn't it Jenny?
That stupid candle's ranting on
Excuse me I'd just like to say that I don't feel like singing today. Sorry sorry.
Frank you don't have to sing if you don't want to. It's ok Luv
Thanks Kathy
You've got nice boobs Jenny. Did ya make a wish? You're supposed to make a wish.
Poppycock
I wont go to depression
Look Sweetheart. Depression's good for you. None of us want to go to depression.
I enjoy depression Kathy. Do you like depression Mike?

I get a bit anxious about it. Nah I don't think I'll
go. Think I'll do me journal
Look here Luv, you're a very nice person but
you've got to go to depression. Ok, that's it
All right, all right Kathy, but I must say I'd rather
be here having a party with me mates.

Judith Dowling

Request

Write me a poem
of grandeur and lust,
of sorrow and woe
a tribute if you must
love is an isn't
and was what it will be
a future past tensor
of something I don't see.
Never shall I be able
to put into words
the anguish I feel
as I write
To love not love at all
is the shame I have to bear
choking on emotions inside
wondering will the reader care
Shame doesn't matter
as pain is all I feel
memories enter
& hearts turn to steel.

Foti

MOON

Two gentle charms, twins of sky, lay hiding in the moon
Each with their own destiny, yet neither of them knew
When the moon was bright and full of light streaming silently from Sun
A chance to see what lay outside their oracle abode had come
'Let's go out and see what sparkles in our place of night
And hear those bells claim praise and sing to angels' one said with expectant delight
'I long to know what life is, will you stay to go on shining in Mother Moon for me?'
'But here we are together, we are each other's love and light Moon's hopeful beam
What if the dark is cold and life is sad, how do I bring you home my precious, if you fade
Will you see me as you get closer to Suns many tomorrows of days?'
Please stay, my only one, stay here, amongst Gods promises above
We are here because with both hearts we are the light for Moons love
Let's ask the angels if we should stay, not just one here and one gone
'But I yearn to see and be, to have and to play
Surely I will be welcomed by all those who see us appear at the end of day'
'My lunar twin, I don't know if I have enough love on my own
What if Moons Shadow should cross, what if God calls us to heaven, what should I say?'

'It's God's word that I long to follow, let me go my darling, and be part of tomorrow.'
So Moon was left with one otherworldly sprite, keeping it warm, keeping it bright
As Moon's child came down from the sky, the horizon of Suns dawn had begun to rise
All the colours of life smiled and greeted their new friend
Dancing in Sun's changing moods, through the day they laughed and sang,
But Moon's child lost sight of sister, she had gone in the other side of the world called night

Sister couldn't call out, she couldn't shine, she didn't have enough love to keep Moon alight
When day ended Moon's child wanted to go home, back to God's heavenly jewel in the sky
But she couldn't see Moon anymore, her eyes had changed and she became afraid,
The angels on the stars could only watch, they couldn't sing to Moon's child, only pray
She felt alone for the first time in night and needed to kiss the Moon and say
'We are forever together in our love my precious sister'
By fate their prayers had come to God at the same time "Keep us together, we are sisters
Please give us our own light, if we are caught in tomorrows down there or here in sky's night
Please give sister my love and light I promise to be brave in the days of tomorrows Sun'
Every night our guardian angels are kissing the stars and sending us one
Moon's sister prayed 'You are great and can see us although we're apart

I promise I will watch for you in all the days of life, as they end and as they start,
I was adventurous but I know my sister is shy, I promise I will watch for her in infinity's sky,
I ask for many tomorrows so I can see her before they begin and again when they end
Please tell her she is so beautiful to me,
Beautiful to the night, and I love my best friend
All we know is each other, and we both need our love to keep each other alive
Keep us together in that love, always, even if we are now kept on life's different sides.

Suzanne Siebert

Like a ripple in some stream

Like a ripple in some stream
I let your current take me down
Way past my consciousness of dream
Too hard to prove within your sound.
Too hard to breathe I close my eyes
As coloured lights explode in air
Is this how life expires and dies?
Or is it love that floats nowhere?
Or is it time that broke my heart
When indeed better tried than you
To lure my trust with such, is art
It seems, too pure when not so true.
It seems so simple all these lines
That make up how I yearn
So easy weaving past the mines
And yet, I burn.

Andrew Lewis

Clap Back

If the thought of me truly makes you sick;
stop writing songs and stories about all you say
I 'did'
And while I'm here, you can stop acting so damn
innocent.

You want to complain and moan about your
broken heart,
Take it up with God, you aren't a bloody star,
flex on this one and pump this chick
but we both know you aren't worth it

see you aren't the only one who can spin a
rhyme,
It's not some Godly talent and now you are out
of time

It's been nine months now, will you just let it go
you're nothing but a self-entitled country
bumpkin
with a swollen ego.

Amanda Divers

I hear the silence all the time

I hear the silence all the time
When a conversation erases
The fluidity of reason
In between words and phrases.

A pause almost unnoticed
Yet rings in my ears
Long after, and waits again
Through endless years.

Old thoughts that tend to hang and leave
Baggage from another source
Unchallenged links to pain and grief
Though dormant, still in force.

Behind some walls that I have built
I believe, are ladders I could climb
To find that space in peace and quiet
Where no silence marks my time.

Peter Levy

I intermingle with the living

I intermingle with the living, surging beside the current
Of thoughts within motives, agendas beyond belief
Where those of much courage, or shadowed despair,
Lurch to and fro with rationale, as I glean like a thief.
Forsaking form and rhythm to be original, even true
One word enjoins another, in a way so foreign and free
Cowering no-one, as if already drained by the perceived vigour
Pointless in execution, saline drenched, futile.
Except to me.
Except to me.

Elizabeth MacGregor

Speak To Me

My spanking new printer and
my erstwhile modem refuse
to communicate. Out of sync
like lovers at loggerheads.
Though I psyched myself up
for the techno turmoil with a
sickly smile pasted to my face;
I tried to make it real, really.
The new printer complied with
every press of its buttons but
point blank refused to talk to
the old modem or vice versa or
perhaps it was mutual distaste or
they just don't understand each other.
It's time to cross the Rubicon of
Telstra Platinum where people
with calm voices mould machines
to their bidding all day. The sweet- voiced young
fellow tries every
techno twist to pair the printer with its
mate. Still they won't relate.
I keep my cool and while I wait I type this patient
verse upon my pad.
Ah! Another modem is on its way, youthful and
ready to give the green light,
to leave its imprint on the printer
who has clearly been awaiting a new sleek
model who is on its wavelength.

Ann Simic

The Biographer

Whatever happened to the Ugly Sisters?
Well may you ask!
Aha! You'll have to read my biography
I'll tell you so much …
The truth, only the truth.
Firstly there's Voilenta
The elder one, that's me
I suffered an awful breakdown
After the wedding …
After the cleaning girl Cindy flaunted herself
Wed that fabulously rich newspaper mogul
And drove off in a solid gold Ferrari
Wearing crystal shoes studded with diamonds
It should have been me!

I eventually got over the mogul
I bought (thanks to Mummy)
A nice little business in undies
"Ladies Intimate Apparel"
Knickers, bras, teddies and such
For footballer's wives and footballers
It was all a huge success
Considering I once got an axe through my head.

Truth, truth. Let me see
Let me behold it before my eyes
It's not that I was ugly at all
Oh no, no, no
All that was just a symbol
Of what a terrible childhood can do
Some upstart reporter got it wrong.

Poor Mummy
Even before her rigor mortis
Daddy married that pathetic woman
And of course she had to produce
Their damnable Petronella
She was only a half and so ugly
Drove a Porsche at twelve
To Monte Carlo on Saturday nights
Read all about it.
And here's another snippet or two
She, the little half, Petty, got the wrong man
Four times
She ended up in cement (thanks to husband three)
After the lobotomy failed
After she'd snipped off her ten little pinkies
With Daddy's secateurs.

My own research shows that Cindy
Fell off her shoes and lost both her feet
The mogul? Ha! He lost all his hair.
I've a man who's going to marry me ...
After my next facelift.
I'll sit as I write, looking perfectly lovely
In the tower of our amazing McMansion
Overlooking the sea.

Judith Dowling

Taste is Everything

Aspirations mixed with doubt.
Sight matters the least,
yet we spend the most effort on how others perceive us.
It's feelings that matter.
When I see someone,
it's not their symmetry or beauty, it's their expression looking at me.
Are her eye's smiling?
What emotions is she feeling
– is she conveying to me?
Taste is everything.
Anyone can look at her.
Sometimes we may see aspirations filled with doubt.
That's vision's fragile nature.
Sight pales compared to other senses. And yet to gaze at her and perceive her emotion of love – means everything to me! That is her beauty.
Anyone can hear her. Her soft, warm, soul melting sweet tones as she speaks to me convey how she feels for me. For to hear her tone of love is everything to me.
That is her beauty.
Anyone can smell her. Perfume fragrances please the mind, yet it is her smell when near, her warm breath, her lightly perspiring back so near, the smell of home when my face is engulfed in her luscious hair. Being close enough to smell her so, is everything. That is her beauty.
Anyone can touch her.

To shake her gentle hand, pat her on the back. She brings warmth and caring to those she touches, and to the items she handles. Yet when she holds me, caresses me and I her, emotions of love calm my nervous soul, bring rest to my tired mind, and peace. That is her beauty. Yet, only I can taste her. This is ours and ours alone. True love is found in this of all senses. Nor food, nor drink taste as the emotion of love, when flesh and spirit are shared. That is the beautifulness that her love reserves for only me, letting me know that we are one.

Foti

Testing the water

I wake with my mind already blank and empty, yet without space for thought
I take my first steps slowly, my feet bare
As though my cold toes are testing the water, of today's unknowns
On a day I don't care to have because even that feels wrong
I feel so numb, but I feel too much, beyond a reason or reality of sense
With it comes a stark reality of new confusion
Knowing that now this is how my days will always begin
The words 'this is real' emerge along with 'this is how it will be'
I could drown seeing with eyes that are crying tides of tears
Not in the ocean though, that's just life and life's been rough
But it isn't nearly powerful enough, and I've swum that sea for years
Emotions range and without warning they change, only to change again
This is my ocean of regret and love is as wild as the wind wants
And as random as a current chooses to be
Despite the thrill I know I could have running away from the tumbling wash
I won't venture further than the shore
I won't be bracing or slightly holding back from the waves about to crash
Then chase them out again, just as children do and have always done

I only watch it fade into a white, wet salt that will just land on sand
There is no breeze, time or tide and for me there is no desire to run
Instead an overwhelming haze rushes through me and it's already won
It comes when I wake, with my mind empty and blank
My feet bare I slowly take my first step
I will always be testing the water

Suzanne Siebert

If she only knew

If she only knew my thoughts
And the fear of the secrecy
While my mind does cartwheels on the street
I smile and look innocent.
Longings of pure lust
So few beliefs to set free
There is betrayal on many levels
But never with she.

Andrew Lewis

I Had A Dream

I had a dream we never met.
I never memorised your birthday, I never gave myself to you.
I had a dream, and I was still whole.
I was healed, I wasn't scared anymore.
I still loved endlessly, I still loved loud.
It didn't take endless hours to fall asleep, and being alone wasn't a chore.
I had a dream I never met you.
I never went with my sister to that place
I never fell for those kind captivating eyes
I had a dream I didn't miss you.
Somehow I think, like everything, I was just the one who loved you more.
I made a wish today, a wish we never met.

Amanda Divers

Still there

The whisper through the leaves
Unspoken thoughts
Barren rivers, broken bushes
Charred memories.
Timeless prints upon the sand
Valueless?
Messages from beyond
Not understood.
Rocks coloured by the sun
With little meaning
Teachers have all but gone
Forgotten.
And yet I still hear the whisperer
Faintly
On the breeze from ruined trees
Still there.
Still there.
Still there.

Peter Levy

None but the brave

We all stand on the brink of enlightenment
Most of the life we live is pure fiction
Only death is honest and real.
The abyss beckons every day without agendas
Numbers disappear without questions
I'm not sure how ready I am.
You are still and fragile as guardian of the bridge
Short fragments reason my soul
None but the brave step forward.

Elizabeth MacGregor

In the Pink on the Mexican/US Border

Newton nailed it with talk of action and reaction:
reciprocity echoed in bright pink seesaws
slashing Trump's triumphal dismal wall where
mother split from child may connect
as they fly and descend to earth.
Where anyone can laugh across that
dreary dumb wall and heal hearts
briefly before the inspired installation
is dismantled. Even sentries smile to see
the fleeting joy the artists have enabled.
Squalid deeds trumped by wit and humour
flying in the face of insidious separation:
intent and impact subverted, thumbing
noses at futile fences. A fulcrum balancing
life's ups and downs against the
awful angst of building barriers.

Ann Simic

Belles De Jour

Champagne!
For those wonderful women
Les marchande de mode
Hattie Head, Chapeaux Cherie
Madelaine Hattier and all
They deserved medals
For their service to women
Forget the horses
Voyer vous, vive l' elegance
At the Spring Racing Carnival.

They make short women tall
With a phallic crown erect
With a plume or two
With a twirl and a flick
Reaching up and over
Tickling the noses of the tallest men
Signalling Look at me! Look!

See the dollops of blanc-mange
Piled onto a plate
Spooned on to many a head
Like faire les amoureux, gateaux delice
Cuisine marveilleux for a grande apetit
La haute couture
La horticulture!

Hats
They can make older women young again
From a distance
If they peep out furtively
From under the shade of flippy brims
With decoy spring gardens atop
If they disappear into the crowd
As quickly as they came.

See how they make shy girls laugh
Plain girls pretty
Pretty girls beautiful
Beautiful girls heaven sent
Les Belles de jour!
Dressed up from heel to head
Standing in groups, whispering
About the passing parade
"Doesn't she just look a sight!"
Assured of their own gorgeousness
Flaunting about in their hats.

Judith Dowling

Erase my mind

Erase me
Don't want to be me any more
Tired of my shortcomings and failings
Tired of this mind
Want to be a clean slate with
few   simple rules and a blank brain
to rapidly   develop into the person I could be, but not me,
Not this dead end street of a person
But an open highway
God, family, friends, fitness and fun
A future full of fantasy come true
Simple, solid. No spasms of regret.
Just smooth soothing soberness
Stillness and attention.
Perhaps even a smile
Focused, productive, powerful
On   The Path   I really want to be   on
Not this path full of excuses
Helping others lost down this path
Healing and resetting our lost, faulty algorithms
Through wisdom and purpose   driven by unrelenting passion
Aliveness, fully human, on the path to Theosis
Knowing we are earning an unimaginably good future,
Living the best now, and and and, reset me
Let me restart   reboot   impress me   with a new me.

Foti

Shadows

Shadows are like secrets, we all have one.
Some are dark, but disperse, others are unrelenting
Following closely on a trail I am unaware I'm making –
Changing by the clouds, changing along my path,
Yes, shadows will come, so will secrets, time creates them.
Secrets are genuinely disguised and shadows crawl steadfast in their length
But both are very alive in their profound silence
Soon both will whisper to me again, be it may or be it when-
It's only lost truth, and lost light, that brings them into being
Ironically, it's only in truth and light that I can see them.
Hiding in a shadow is an easy escape
I can disappear among its cast illusions.
It's being in front of them that is exhausting-
Presenting a face, my face, and to stand there
Before a constantly evolving imitation of my form
Shadows and secrets extend into a dinged, clinging yet intangible thing
A depth of no colour, of no sound,
Keep constantly there and aware, on guard but show nothing
Because they will and still hold you as they have always done
Shadows are like secrets, we all have one.

Suzanne Siebert

Who am I?

I don't blame anyone anymore, because
We are all trapped inside a similar lie
And who am I to shout freedom words
To you, my love, yeh, who am I?
We're still the same, nothing's changed
Don't panic yet, my job's still fine
It's the point of things that now comes clearer
And it's not an easy think sometimes in my mind.
It's like I've lost the plot of things, or found it,
On how you all expect me to be
But I've reached that point that had to happen
In peeling off the debris, just to find me.

Andrew Lewis

The Devil Cries

Where faux furs and thunder claps are lying here for days
and where am I? The darkness here is spread across the glade
for you my love, my debonair id live a thousand lives
each and every one of them till I settled at your side
A wood chipped night,
a deathly fright
for those left out to freeze
nor you, or I, or anything else
could put this tainted heart at ease
A dark winged bat comes beaming down
swallowing my life whole
the devil cries, and here I lie deep within my soul.

Amanda Divers

Just now! Just you!

There is no future, We drift inside space
Illusion in delusion, We stumble with grace.
There are no country borders
No right and no wrong
No god and no heaven
No dream that lasts long
There is nothing outside us
No friend and no foe
No winning and losing
No debts that we owe.
There is no wisdom
No reason to be
No purpose in living
Just mirrors of me.
There is no salvation
No hope in the end
No saviour to pray for
No soul to defend.
There is no protection
We die and we grieve
Wasteful of moments
Then nothing to leave.
There is no forever
Love fails in its brew
No yesterday or tomorrow
Just now! Just you!

Peter Levy

Perhaps

Perhaps, is too strong a word within the confines of my misery
I will always tear the magic from your heart
Maybe in the light that I have hidden is an answer for the blind
But I am like the river flowing out from start to start.
If you plan to understand and be the one to mirror beauty
In reflection of a world where love is all
A kindness in the wisdom has the strength to bear the burden
Slowly, yet beyond fair reason's lonely wall.
Perhaps, is too weak a thought for minds of conscience to respect
Some cling onto words that cannot ever be
A fool has walked that road to brand some nonsense logic
And there you are, a smarter man than me.
It's a paradox at times to justify and make it real hypocrisy
Whereby time I let my participation lapse
I see the world so differently through eyes of mediocrity
Forever stumbling in your debt, perhaps.

Elizabeth MacGregor

www.ingramcontent.com/pod-product-compliance
Lightning Source LLC
Chambersburg PA
CBHW031429290426
44110CB00011B/592